THE

JAMIE JOHNSON

SERIES

WRITTEN BY
DAN FREEDMAN

NIMBLEFEET
PUBLISHERS

Published by Nimble Worldwide.

Adapted from the original edition of Jamie Johnson: Born to Play.
Text © Dan Freedman, 2015.This adaptation first published by Nimble Feet LLC in 2015.
This edition published by Nimble Feet in 2023.

The right of Dan Freedman to be identified as author of this work has been asserted by him.

ISBN 978 1 7384524 0 8
All rights reserved.

This is a work of fiction. Names, characters, places, incidents and dialogues are products of the author's imagination or are used fictitiously. Any resemblance to actual people, living or dead, events or locales is entirely coincidental.

As is the case with any sport involving speed, agility, balance, and environmental factors, soccer poses some inherent risk. Specifically, the soccer skills described in *Born to Play* can be dangerous if attempted. The author and publisher advise readers to take full responsibility for their safety and they do not recommend readers attempt the skills described in the book without the proper supervision from an accredited coach or guardian. Additionally, the author and publisher suggest readers not take risks beyond their personal level of experience, aptitude, training, and comfort level. The author and publisher are not responsible for any injury incurred as a result of readers attempting any skills associated with and/or mentioned in The Jamie Johnson Series.

The Jamie Johnson logo is a trademark of Nimble Feet Worldwide Limited
www.nimblefeet.co
Cover photo elements ©iStockphoto/Nikada, ©iStockphoto/svengine
Design and formatting by Jennifer Ferguson.

10 9 8 7 6 5 4 3 2 1

www.jamiejohnson.soccer

Praise for The Jamie Johnson Series

"I almost feel like I am Jamie Johnson now"
JUDE BELLINGHAM

"You'll read this and want to get out there and play"
STEVEN GERRARD

"True to the game... Dan knows his soccer"
OWEN HARGREAVES

"An inspiring read for all soccer fans"
GARY LINEKER

"Jamie could go all the way"
JERMAIN DEFOE

"Pure class—brings the game to life"
OWEN COYLE

"I love reading about soccer and it
doesn't get much better than this"
JOE HART

"Had me flipping the pages faster than lightning"
SPORTS ILLUSTRATED KIDS

About The Jamie Johnson Series

The Jamie Johnson Series follows the life of a boy who dreams of being a famous professional soccer player. We first meet Jamie Johnson in fifth grade, and we follow every step of his journey from school all the way through to soccer's biggest stage, the World Cup, and even beyond.

These bestselling novels originated in the United Kingdom, where their author, Dan Freedman, lives. Dan is thrilled to be bringing this new version of The Jamie Johnson Series to the United States, written exclusively for the American audience, beginning here with *Born to Play*. Remember, *Born to Play* is just the beginning of Jamie's story, so look out for the next chapter in The Jamie Johnson Series—coming soon!

About the Author

DAN FREEDMAN grew up wanting to be a professional soccer player. That didn't happen. But he went on to become a top soccer journalist, personally interviewing the likes of Cristiano Ronaldo, Lionel Messi and David Beckham. He uses his passion and knowledge of the game to write the hugely popular series of Jamie Johnson soccer novels. When he is not writing, Dan delivers talks and workshops for schools. He discusses his experiences in soccer and his career as a writer, passing on one simple message to kids everywhere: *Go For Your Goals!* Dan still plays soccer whenever he can.

www.jamiejohnson.soccer

THE JAMIE JOHNSON SERIES

Born to PLAY

The start of a soccer legend

A NOVEL BY

DAN FREEDMAN

NIMBLEFEET
PUBLISHERS

Table of Contents

FRIDAY

1

The Soccer Computer

Jamie lined up the strike and turned on the soccer computer in his mind.

He zoomed in on the target, instantly analyzing and calculating the distance, power, angle and velocity required.

Then, he stepped confidently and angrily forward and swept his foot through the ball with every bit of dynamic force that existed in his body.

He watched the ball take off and fire through the air like a missile, whistling fast and hard, heading directly for its target with inexorable accuracy.

Jamie knew his strike would hit the mark. It always did. That soccer computer in his brain was his most reliable and devastating weapon.

But right now, it wasn't the goal he was aiming for.

Drake Staunton was standing with the rest of his crew by the side of the playground. They really thought they owned this school. They really thought they could terrorize and belittle Jamie just because he was new, just because he was American.

They were wrong. He would never accept their taunts. Never let them win.

Drake Staunton was just tipping his head back, laughing at some other kids that he was bullying, when Jamie's shot struck him, full on, in the side of the face, causing Drake to turn around instantly with anger to see who dared to hit him with the soccer ball.

He didn't have to search long. Jamie Johnson was standing there on the other side of the playground staring straight back at him.

I'm right here, Jamie was saying with his eyes. *I'm not going anywhere.*

If Drake wanted to go at it again, Jamie was ready. Any time, any place.

2

The Last Chance

"Oh no," said Karen Johnson, Jamie's mom, seeing the pink slip of paper waiting for her on the kitchen table. "Not again!"

"He deserved it," snarled Jamie. "I'm not scared of him. I'm not going to let him think he's better than me."

Karen Johnson shook her head and rested her chin on her hand. Her skin had lost all its color.

"But, Jamie, this is the third note you've had from the principal since we've arrived. He's losing patience with you. Look, look what he says: *'This is my final warning. If there's another incident of this nature, I'll be forced to take more severe action.'*"

"I'll be forced to take more severe action," Jamie mimicked, putting on his best, fake British accent.

"Oh my God," said Karen, looking at her son as though she did not recognize him. "You really don't care, do you? None of this means anything to you, does it? What's happened to the old Jamie? What's happened to my son? I miss him so much."

Jamie looked at his mom. There was a tear in the corner of her eye. He felt bad. But only for a second.

"He doesn't exist," Jamie snapped, slamming the kitchen door behind him. "Not in this stupid country anyway."

It had been three months since Karen and Jamie Johnson had arrived in England on that flight from their small suburban town in southern Maine. Mike Johnson, Jamie's English grandpa, had met them at the airport and the two adults had been all smiles, pretending everything was fine, even acting like it was a good thing that they had to move to England.

But Jamie hadn't been smiling. What was there to smile about? His dad was in jail. Jamie didn't know all of the details, but he knew it had to do with him using his job at the bank to take money from other people. His mom couldn't face the embarrassment of having their house and all of their possessions taken away, not to mention what everyone in the neighborhood would say about his dad. So, she made the decision to come back to England—to *her* country—and live near her dad for some support and to start a new life.

That was that. No discussion. No explanation. No chance for Jamie to have his say. He was expected to just swallow it.

"You'll love England," she had promised him, trying to make it sound as though this was all good news, that it would be some great adventure. "Everyone will make such a big deal of you because you're American."

Jamie hadn't bought a word of it.

"I'm staying here," he had said. "You're the one that's British. Not me. I'm American. This is my country. This is my home. Why should I be punished for what Dad's done? And you're just scared about what all the other moms will say about you. You're running away! Just admit it.

"You go," he had snapped. "I'm staying."

Of course he couldn't do that. He was a ten-year-old boy. It wasn't his decision to make, so in the end, he had to go with his mom.

He even had to change his last name from Reynolds to Johnson so that he and his mom had the same name. After what his dad had done, his mom wanted to erase every trace of him from their lives, including his name.

So, Karen and Jamie Johnson arrived in England on that bleakly cold November night, three months ago. And, since the moment that Jamie had stepped off that plane, he had not smiled once.

Tough Guy

Jamie sloshed his way slowly up the path to Wheat-lands Primary School, feeling the cold, slushy ice invade his old shoes with each reluctant step.

Even the weather here was half-hearted. Back home, when it snowed, it really snowed. Sometimes they would have 20 inches outside their door and everyone had to stay home for days.

Here, it snowed a bit, then it rained a lot, and at the end, all that was left was this gray, dirty slush that found its way into every part of Jamie's clothing.

Gray and dirty. That was how this school seemed to Jamie. Everything was small, old and boring. Even the playground where they played soccer at recess was nar-row, enclosed in the small school grounds with no real room to run.

Back home, there was light and space. When Jamie thought about being at school, he remembered all the kids smiling, running free. Here in Wheatlands Primary School—even the name was strange—Jamie felt hemmed in. He felt trapped.

Jamie walked into the main entrance of the school and looked at the notice board. The sign was up for the game next week.

Jamie stared at it:

This is the boys' team for the match against Stonecroft on Monday. The biggest game of the year! Bus leaves at 12:45pm, match kicks off at 1:30pm.

Have a good weekend!
Mr. Karenza

1. Bernard Thompson
2. Eric Yerets
3. Mo Salek
4. Harry Shipwright
5. Drake Staunton (captain)
6. David Shultz
7. Dexter Talbot
8. Aaron Cody
9. Kane Talbot
10. Eddie Foreman
11. Jamie Johnson

Sub: Tyler Forbes

"You're an idiot, you know that don't you?"

Jamie looked to his left. It was Alex Crawford, a girl from Jamie's class. She was the one kid in the whole school that seemed to talk to Jamie like he was a normal person.

When he arrived, half of the school had treated Jamie like he was a superstar. Lots of the kids couldn't believe that an American boy was actually at their school and insisted on asking a whole load of the most stupid questions he had ever heard.

"Do all Americans eat hot dogs?"

"If you call crisps chips, then what do you call chips?"

"Do you know Beyonce?"

"How long does it take to walk across America?"

One boy called Hugo Bogson—the geekiest kid in the whole school—had even managed to get it into his head that Jamie had something to do with the CIA!

"I know why you're here," he said to Jamie during recess once, tapping his nose conspiratorially, as though they were sharing come kind of secret.

"CIA business, isn't it? You're here to bring down the Prime Minister aren't you? Don't worry, I won't tell. To be completely honest, I'm not much of a fan of the Prime Minister myself."

Meanwhile, the rest of the kids, like Drake and his goons, seemed to have a problem with Jamie simply because he was American. They mocked his accent at every opportunity. They told him to go home, that he wasn't welcome here. And they tried to fight him, which was why Jamie kept getting into trouble. He had spent more time in the office with Mr. Karenza—the principal—than any other kid. But he did not care. He would not let anyone bully him. Ever.

But Alex Crawford was the one person who seemed to truly accept Jamie. She had never made him feel like an outsider.

"I'm an idiot?" said Jamie, responding to her comment. "Why is that?"

"Because if you keep getting in trouble you'll get banned from playing soccer and you'll miss this," she said, pointing to the details of the game against Stonecroft. Alex was captain of the girls' team. Their line-up had been posted alongside the boys' team.

"Our games against Stonecroft are like the biggest deal! You have no idea what it would mean to this school if we beat them. If you play like you can and score the winning goal, trust me—it'll change everything. You'll be the most popular kid in the whole school. So, I know it's difficult for you—but STAY OUT OF TROUBLE!"

Jamie looked at her and shook his head.

"Who says I want to be popular in this school anyway?" he snorted. "Who says I even care about beating Stonecroft?"

Alex Crawford stared at Jamie and then she laughed.

"You might fool the other kids with your tough guy act, Jamie Johnson, but you don't fool me."

4

Boy in Trouble

It was Friday afternoon—the end of another long, tortuous week—and Jamie was just about to leave the school when he heard a high-pitched scream.

He thought a girl must have hurt herself, but when he looked over to the side of the playground, he saw that the noise was coming from Hugo Bogson.

"Please! Don't!" Hugo was wailing.

Drake Staunton and Tyler Forbes, the two school bullies, were all over Hugo. Not that this was a new development. Hugo was probably the only kid that they targeted more than Jamie. Their problem with Jamie was that he was new and he had taken Tyler Forbes' place on the soccer team. Their problem with Hugo was that he was different, just plain different.

With thick black curly hair and huge purple glasses,

Hugo acted and spoke like he was some kind of ten–year–old science professor. He even claimed to be working on a time machine at his house. He was a truly unusual kid. Not that that gave Drake and Tyler the right to mess with him like this. Tyler was holding him down, squeezing his neck, while Drake seemed to be putting something in his hair. Hugo sounded as though he was in real pain.

"Please don't! I've got ballet tonight!" Hugo was screaming in terror. But it was too late. Drake was already squeezing maple syrup all over his hair.

"Oh!" cried Hugo. They had taken his glasses off too, and he was pretty much blind without them. "Oh no, what have you done to me?"

The syrup was oozing down the side of Hugo's cheek now as his two assailants collapsed into laughter. Today had been Pancake Day at school and the two jackals had obviously stolen the leftover food from the cafeteria.

"That's just for starters, you nerd!" jeered Drake before taking a whole box of eggs out of his bag. "Now for the main course!"

"Oh, you can't! Please!!" begged Hugo as Drake opened the box while a laughing Tyler held the victim down. "My parents and I are going to the science museum after ballet and they'll never let me in if you do this... the eggs will mix with the syrup and congeal and I'll..."

"Shut your face!" bellowed Drake, raising two eggs

above Hugo's head.

"Leave him alone," shouted Jamie, suddenly appearing. "Leave him alone now."

The way Jamie saw it, he was from America and Hugo... well, Hugo was from another galaxy. But the point was, they were both outsiders. They had that in common.

"Oh, yeah, Yankee boy," barked Drake. "Or what? What you gonna do about it?"

"Make you sorry you ever laid a finger on him," replied Jamie.

But Drake Staunton let out the most evil laugh that he could and then brought his egg-carrying fist down towards Hugo's helpless head.

"No!!!" Hugo wailed but, just before the impact was made, Jamie flashed across the ground and grabbed Drake's hand, pinning his wrist behind his back. It was one of the martial arts moves he had learned in his after school karate club back home.

Tyler Forbes immediately left Hugo and ran towards Jamie but Jamie tripped him up on the way, and then sat on Tyler's back so he couldn't get up. Then, while he was still sitting on Tyler, he squeezed Drake's wrist even harder, twisting his arm even further behind his back.

"Now," said Jamie. "Do you wanna say sorry to Hugo?"

Drake shook his head. Jamie applied even more pressure.

"Ahhh!" Drake yelled, dropping the eggs. "Leave me alone!"

"Not until you say sorry to Hugo. You know, he might not be able to go to ballet now because of you."

"I'm... sorr-eeee," Drake moaned as Jamie twisted his arm to an even more agonizing position.

"Good," said Jamie, releasing Drake and getting up off Tyler's back. "That's all you had to say."

Drake and Tyler looked at Jamie as though he was some kind of alien and scampered off out of the school grounds.

"There you go," said Jamie, handing Hugo back his glasses.

"Oh, thank you!" Hugo gushed. "You practically saved my life, Agent Johnson!"

"We'll get you back, you Yankee freak!" Drake shouted, once he and Tyler were far enough away for Jamie not to race after them.

"Looking forward to it already!" Jamie yelled in their direction, bending down to pick up an egg and hurl it in their direction.

The egg narrowly missed, smashing into the window instead, but it didn't matter. Jamie had done what he wanted. Those fools wouldn't be messing with Hugo Bogson again for a while.

SATURDAY

5

Tell It Like It Is

"Grandpa Mike will be here in a minute. Are you ready?" Jamie's mom called up the stairs. "And make sure you take your warmest coat! It's raining!"

"Fine!" Jamie grunted back down the stairs. If he had a dollar for every time his mom had told him to wear a coat because it was raining since they had arrived...

"Have a good time, you two," Jamie's mom said as they left the house. "And Dad, please don't get any of your secret fish and chip meals on the way home—I want him to have an appetite for his dinner."

Jamie's grandpa, Mike, had been promising to take Jamie to a Premier League soccer match for the last two months but every game seemed to be sold out. Today they finally had tickets to see their most local team, Hawkstone United, and Jamie could tell his mom was hoping this would be a chance for him and his grandpa to develop a proper relationship.

"They haven't really hit it off yet," Jamie had heard her say over over the phone to one of her friends back home. "But I know he really needs some male company."

The problem was Jamie barely knew his grandpa. Sure, he had come out to the States a couple of times when Jamie was really young—and he was the one that had bought Jamie his first soccer ball—but, in truth, they had never really spent much time together.

And yet, now that Jamie and his mom were living in England, she expected Jamie to suddenly think this guy was the best person in the world. But it didn't work like that. When he came to think of it, all Jamie really knew about his grandpa was that when he was a teenager, he had been a professional soccer player for Hawkstone himself. But then had torn the cruciate ligament in his knee when he was 17, which caused him agonizing pain.

To make matters worse, he had been so desperate to play again that he tried to make his comeback way too early, before his knee had fully healed, and ended up damaging himself even more severely. This all meant that he had to retire from professional soccer at the age of 19. His career was over before it even really began. These days, he was a taxi cab driver.

"How's school?" asked Jamie's grandpa as they walked to the stadium.

"Fine," managed Jamie.

"No stories to tell me?"

"No," responded Jamie.

They carried on walking in silence. Jamie could see his grandpa's mind working, trying to come up with a conversation topic.

"Your mom tells me that next week you're playing against Stonecroft," he said, cheerfully. "You know how badly your school will want to beat them, don't you? If you can beat them, it'll make such a diff–"

"I know!" said Jamie, cutting off his grandpa. "I get it."

Jamie's grandpa stopped walking. He stared at Jamie. Then he put his hands on his grandson's shoulders.

"This isn't working is it?" he said. "It hasn't worked since you arrived... here's me being all happy and jovial and there's you being... well, like a kid who's just been moved to another country, to another continent."

"I don't care," said Jamie, avoiding eye contact as they spoke. "Makes no difference to me."

"Well," said Jamie's grandpa. "I know that back home you lived in your lovely big house. You had your pool, you had your friends, you had everything you wanted... and then, one day—snap—it's all over and you have to leave everything you've ever known."

Jamie just stared at the ground.

"How about you and me do things differently from now on?" Jamie's grandpa suggested. "I think I'd like it if you called me Mike instead of Grandpa. I'd like to be your friend, if you'll let me.

"And, in return, I promise that, instead of pretending everything's perfect, you and me will just tell it like it is.

"Pals?" offered Mike, holding out his hand.

Jamie looked at him. He wasn't sure. He couldn't afford to allow people into his life if they were going to let him down. But at least his grandpa—Mike—was being honest, or was starting to. Jamie had respect for that.

He shook Mike's hand.

A Tribal Game

"Here," said Mike, ushering Jamie in front of him as they lined up to enter the stadium through the turnstiles.

Jamie was happy to be in his grandfather's protection. There were so many people and there was a sense of tension all around. This was not what Jamie had expected. Not what he had expected at all.

Back home, when Jamie went to watch Major League Soccer games, the atmosphere had been like a party. Jamie, his dad, his friends from school and their brothers, sisters and parents had all gone along together as one big group.

They would arrive at the stadium two or three hours before the game to tailgate, play some soccer, practice their skills, have a barbeque and even make new friends. It felt like an amazing day out, even before the game began. That was one of the really special aspects of going to a soccer game back home—how everyone mixed together and just had a good time.

But walking into this English stadium today, Jamie noticed there was a different vibe. It felt as though this match was the single most important thing going on in the whole world.

"Football—as we call it—is different here than in other countries," said Mike, responding to Jamie's bemused face as they found their seats. "A famous Scottish coach even once said that soccer over here is not a matter of life and death... it's much, much more important than that."

"Right," smiled Jamie, looking around. "Who are they?" he asked, pointing at the several thousand fans in the far corner of the stadium.

They were all jumping up and down and singing like madmen. Some of them even had no shirts on, despite the fact that it was freezing.

"Those are the away fans," said Mike. "They come to support the other team. They travel with them all over the world. The best way I can describe it to you is that fans of different teams are like tribes. You are born into one and that is you. That is your tribe for the rest of your life. The game goes back to the 1800s over here. It's been this way for a very long time."

Jamie shook his head. So this was English soccer. This was English *football*. Thousands of obsessed fans shouting and supporting their tribe, with all the passion and thunder of a battle.

He looked at the gladiators down on the field. He sensed a shiver of anticipation flood around the ground.

He could get used to this.

7

In the Blood

"So you actually played on that field?" Jamie asked Mike, beginning to see his grandpa in an entirely new light. He had been down on that battlefield. He had been one of the warriors. One of the leaders of the tribe.

Mike nodded.

"I played 54 times for the Hawks," he said. "I would have played 1,000 times if only my body had let me. Even now, when I'm watching a game, in my mind I still feel like I could play. I still feel like I have this understanding of where the ball should be and how it should be played. I can see it all so clearly. Does that make sense?"

"Sure does," said Jamie, recognizing a description

that sounded very much like the soccer computer in his own head.

"So what was it like?" he asked. "What did it actually feel like being out there?"

"The most electric moments of my life," said Mike. "I would give anything in the world to get out there again. To experience that feeling. Can you imagine what it's like, Jamie? That rush of energy. That raw passion. That moment of ecstasy when your score a goal and 40,000 fans all sing your name. Honestly, there's nothing like it in the world. Nothing like it at all."

Jamie nodded. He was starting to understand.

He looked down on the field. The little junior captain was having a shot at the goal and, as the stadium announcer read out his name, the Hawkstone fans gave the kid a warm round of applause.

Jamie started to imagine being down there on the field himself, with the fans cheering *him* on, singing *his* name. He could understand why Mike said there was nothing like it in the world.

"So who makes all the decisions? Who owns all of this?" asked Jamie, taking in the full extent of the majestic old stadium.

Mike opened his coat and took out the program that they had bought near the entrance.

"This man," he said, pointing to an article inside.

Good Afternoon,

Welcome to Cast Creek Stadium, the World Famous Home of Hawkstone United, proudly known as The Nest by our tremendous fans.

This is the start of a busy period for our club. We'll all be back here again on Tuesday night for our big FA Cup game against Foxborough and I'm delighted to say that it's already completely sold out.

With your fantastic support behind us, plus our plans to sign some of the best players from around the world, I believe this club can achieve all its goals.

And, as I always say, I may be the owner, but this will forever be your Club.

Please sing your hearts out for our fabulous players today,

TONY WALSH
Owner, Hawkstone United

Jamie's concentration was broken by the sharp whistle of the referee, calling the captains of the two sides together.

"Who's that?" Jamie asked, pointing to one of the players, a giant hulk of a man.

"Ah," said Mike. "That's Diego Medina, our new captain. What a man. Hey, guess where he's from?"

Jamie shook his head.

"He's American," smiled Mike. "It's an amazing story. He played in college in the States at a very high level, and after he graduated he decided to see if he could make it as a pro here in England. As he traveled around the country, he asked every club he could for a try out. No one was interested. We were the only club that took a look at him and, it turns out, he's the bravest, most dedicated player we've ever had. He's an absolute hero."

"All-American hero!" said Jamie.

He had been listening with great concentration to every word that Mike had said. Now, as the Hawkstone supporters sang *"One Diego Medina! There's only one Diego Mediinaaa!"* over and over, Jamie's grandpa explained that this was a chant reserved only for the most respected players in the team.

As he watched Diego Medina preparing to take the kick-off for Hawkstone United in the Premier League, Jamie thought about his own soccer computer. He thought about the fact that he had always been able to do what he wanted with a soccer ball. And he thought about the fact that when he ran with the ball, and put on his turbo sprint, no one could match him. No one could touch him.

This was something he had been born with. Soccer was in his blood and Jamie didn't have to look very far to know where it came from.

"You know what, Mike?" said Jamie. "Back home, whenever people saw how fast I was and what I could do with a ball, they all used to say that when I grow up, I should play in the NFL. And my track coach at school, he always told me that I should concentrate on my running, so that I could get to the Olympics. It felt as though people were always trying to convince me to do something other than soccer."

"That wouldn't happen here," laughed Mike. "Soccer's number one here. If you've got a talent for soccer, you play it. End of story."

Jamie nodded. He stared around this magical stadium, and as he did so, the very beginning of a plan started to hatch in his mind.

"How do you sign for a pro soccer club over here?" Jamie asked Mike.

"You get in line with just about every other kid in the country!" Mike answered.

"No, I mean it," said Jamie. "How does a kid like me get to play for a club like Hawkstone United?"

Mike looked into Jamie's eyes. He saw his grandson was serious.

"Do you realize what you are asking?" Mike said. "Do you realize that Hawkstone play in the Premier League? Do you know how long and hard the journey is for any player to reach the Premier League? It's the soccer equivalent of climbing Mount Everest."

"I understand," said Jamie. "But *you* did it so you can tell me how. Where do I start? Where do I go?"

Mike nodded. It was almost as though, on some level, he had been waiting his whole life for someone to ask him this question.

"You start the journey just like any other," said Mike. "Begin with a first step. Start with your school team. Win your games, inspire your teammates, show people your true ability and dedicate yourself to working hard and improving every single day to make your dream come true ... to climbing that mountain."

"But what about the clubs?' asked Jamie. "When will I be ready to sign for a club?"

"Trust me," smiled Mike. "These clubs know about every single kid in the country. That's their job. If you're good enough and when you're ready, *they* will come and find *you*..."

SUNDAY

8

Out of the Ordinary

Jamie turned on the computer and logged into his email. He had to borrow his mom's laptop because in this house, they only had one computer between them.

Back home, or rather, back in *America*—Jamie knew soon he would have to stop calling the States home—he and his dad had a whole basement to themselves with a pool table, a huge TV screen for the Internet and movies and even a couple of arcade games, which his friends loved to play when they came over.

Here it was different. It was just him and his mom and their bedrooms were so close sometimes he could hear her crying at night.

As for having friends over, Jamie hadn't invited anyone from his new school back to his house yet. He would be way too embarrassed. Where would they even sit? There was only just enough space for him in his room, let alone someone else. And anyway, who would he invite? Hugo Bogson, the eccentric kid who was a mixture between Harry Potter and a crazy science professor?

Perhaps the only person he would like to invite to his house would be Alex Crawford. They hadn't even talked that much yet but, in a way, that didn't seem to matter. They understood each other. And besides, Jamie liked the way she always called him an idiot with that mischievous smile of hers.

He checked his emails and looked at some of the viral videos that his pals back home had sent. There was one of a goat from Hungary skateboarding which really cracked him up—but all the while, it was soccer that was swirling around his mind.

Jamie checked all the latest MLS scores and reports and shook his head; some of these matches that he was missing out on sounded incredible, and more and more younger players were getting their chance all the time.

Beckham and Henry—two absolute world legends—had both played in MLS, and others had followed like Kaka, Rooney, Zlatan and Pirlo. But now it was all about the next generation. He wished he could be there to see them play. *Typical!* Jamie thought to himself. *I leave the States and a whole new group of young players arrive!*

He closed his eyes and imagined having the soccer career of his dreams. He would win all the trophies club soccer had to offer and then, one day, he would even play for the States in the World Cup. He would be the new star soccer player that all the kids in America would be excited about watching. That was his goal. That was the mountain he had to climb.

Mike had told Jamie that if he was serious about climbing that mountain, his school matches would be the first step. Jamie thought about the big game that he would be playing against Stonecroft the next day. He was playing in attack, on the left wing. That was his favorite position. From there, he could cause damage to any opposition. He could beat players on the dribble or cut in and score himself. But if he really wanted to catch the Premier League clubs' attention, he would need to do more than score an ordinary goal. He would have to produce something special. Something out of the ordinary.

Jamie opened up a new tab on his browser and typed the words "bicycle kick."

Loads of videos were returned, showing all sorts of players scoring the most spectacular bicycle kick goals. Ronaldo, Messi, Maradona, Pele, Neymar... they were all there. But the best was by a player called Marco Van Basten from way back in 1986, for a Dutch team called Ajax. He was playing against Den Bosch, another team from the Netherlands. The way that man scored this goal—striking the ball ferociously while he was pretty much upside down in the air, curling it all the way into the top corner—just blew Jamie's mind.

He shook his head and allowed himself to imagine emulating Van Basten's feat in the game against Stonecroft. Over and over, he replayed the pictures, seeing himself strike the ball, just like Van Basten, into the top corner of Stonecroft's goal.

It would be incredibly difficult to pull it off. But not impossible. Not for Jamie. At school, kids like Hugo Bogson boasted about the fact that they had photographic memories—that they could look at a page in a book once and then be able to recall every word without making a mistake.

Jamie didn't have a photographic memory. But he did have a soccer-graphic memory. Someone only had to show him how to do a skill once and that was it—he would have it down.

Jamie altered his search from "bicycle kick" to "how to do a bicycle kick." Immediately several videos popped up. He picked one of a young German kid, who seemed to know what he was doing, explaining how to perfect the art.

"You've just got to relax," said the boy, as he looked at the camera, bouncing a ball on the ground. *"It's all in the timing..."*

Then the boy proceeded to demonstrate several per-fect bicycle kicks, all the while talking to the camera about what he was doing.

"As the ball comes to you, leave your kicking leg on the ground, and jump into the air, leading with your other leg," he said.

"Then keep your eyes completely fixed on the ball, right through until you strike it.

"Strike the ball with your laces... and still keep your eyes on it!

"Then, after you've made your shot, just use your arms to break your fall. That way, you'll be up quickly

to celebrate your goal!"

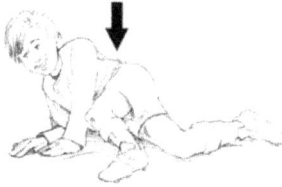

Jamie watched the video five times just to make sure he had it in his head. Then he shut down the laptop, laid on his bed and turned off his light.

His match against Stonecroft was going to kick off in almost exactly 15 hours. And he wanted to use the match to send out a simple message to the Premier League soccer clubs: *COME AND GET ME!*

MONDAY

9

What Money Can't Buy

Jamie raced into school.

He walked into the auditorium for the pep rally, sat himself down next to Alex Crawford, crossed his legs and listened.

He had a new purpose now. There was everything to play for.

"I just want to say a few words about the matches against Stonecroft this afternoon," said Mr. Karenza, bringing up the subject that was already on Jamie's mind.

"Everyone in this room is well aware that these matches mean a lot to this school, to our pride, and to our identity in the area. But I also want you all to remember that you are representing the school when we go there.

"We are sending two teams—the girls, who will be captained by Alex Crawford, and the boys, who will be captained by Drake Staunton. Every one of you will not just be players on the team; you will also be ambassadors for this school. We want to win these games... desperately. But we also need to respect our opponents and ourselves.

"Stonecroft is obviously a very... different school from ours. They may be just down the road, but in some senses they come from a different world. Their wealth means they have different options... different perspectives... but they are not better *people* than us. It's vital that you all remember that.

"Because there is one thing money can't buy. And that is class. I want every student from Wheatlands to show *their* class this afternoon. On and off the field. Make us proud."

Jamie and Alex looked at each other and smiled.

Jamie sensed he was about to take the first step on his journey to the top.

"OK," said Mr. Karenza. "You can all go now....except for Jamie Johnson. I want to see you in my office. Immediately."

10

Crazy

"I presume you know why you're here," said Mr. Karenza sternly.

Jamie shook his head. He had no idea. Something was obviously going on, he just didn't know what.

"It will be so much better for you if you admit it," said Mr. Karenza.

"But I haven't done anything!" responded Jamie, starting to get angry now.

"So you're telling me you didn't throw an egg against the staff room window on Friday afternoon?"

"Oh," said Jamie, suddenly understanding. "Yeah, well... that wasn't my fault, I was just stopping—"

"It's never your fault though, is it, Jamie?" said Mr. Karenza, prodding the point of his pen onto his pad as he spoke. "And you never learn either, do you? What do you think I meant last week when I said that you were on your final warning?"

Mr. Karenza's face reddened as he spoke, the memory of Jamie's many misdemeanors lodged in the forefront of his mind.

"I've come to the end of the line with you, Jamie. I've had enough. This afternoon, I'm taking two of our teams to play Stonecroft, which is the most prestigious school in the whole town. It's a great chance for those kids. And a great responsibility too. There will be lots of people watching, and expecting us to cause trouble because we are the school from the 'poor' neighborhood. Well, that is not going to happen. I am not going to get this wrong. And I am not going to allow *one* person to make the whole school look bad. You will not be representing our school this afternoon. You will not be on that bus."

"What?!" said Jamie panicking. "No way! None of that was my fault!!" Mr. Karenza could not take him off the team. Not today. Today was everything.

"So the egg threw itself at the window, did it?" barked Mr. Karenza. "I've made my decision. And I will not change my mind. Not under any circumstances."

"This is crazy!!" shouted Jamie, standing up and tipping over his chair.

"Well, you better get used to it," responded Mr. Karenza. "Tyler Forbes is going to take your place today and you won't be representing this school for a very, very long time."

Too Brave

"I hate that school, I hate this country, I hate my mom for making me come here and I hate my dad for ruining my life!" Jamie screamed.

Mike said they should tell it how it was and that was what Jamie was doing.

Jamie had kicked his way out of Mr. Karenza's office and past Alex and Hugo, who had been waiting in the hallway to see what happened. Then he stormed out into the playground and leapt right over the fence.

He had run away from school with no intention of ever going back. He wasn't sure where he was going, but his legs had brought him here, to Mike's house, where Jamie banged on the door until it opened.

Since then, Jamie had been venting his anger while Mike watched and listened.

"What am I even doing in this country?" Jamie continued, his voice becoming more and more strained. "No one even asked me. No one ever asked what *I* wanted... well, I want... I want..."

Mike nodded and walked over to give his grandson a hug.

Jamie hit Mike in the chest and shouted.

"I want my old life back!" Jamie yelled."I want to go home!"

And then Jamie did something he had not allowed himself to do for months.

He cried.

* * * *

Mike let Jamie lie down on his bed for half an hour before coming in to say that he had just had a long chat with Mr. Karenza. The principal had promised that if Jamie came back to school quickly, he wouldn't be in trouble.

Jamie said *no way,* but Mike insisted that the longer he left it, the harder it would be.

In the end, Jamie just nodded. He was drained. He was done fighting. They pulled up to the school gates in Mike's cab and sat there for a minute or two, with the engine running.

Jamie had only been gone for a couple of hours but it felt so much longer. He had cried—really cried—while Mike stood hugging him.

Mike told Jamie not to worry, to let it all out. He said that Jamie was brave. Too brave for his own good. That people shouldn't have expected him to handle moving to a different country without any problems. Anyone would find the move difficult, let alone a ten-year-old kid.

"It's OK to be angry, scared and homesick," Mike said. "That's real and I respect you for that. Just know one thing: I'm always on your side."

Jamie looked at Mike uncertainly and unbuckled his seatbelt.

"You'll be fine, Jamie," Mike said. "I promise."

Mike Johnson watched his grandson get out of the car and walk slowly back up the path to the school gates. He tried to put himself in Jamie's shoes. How would *he* have handled losing his dad and his life in one split second? Mike shook his head. The boy was only ten years old.

12

Jumping the Gun

Mr. Karenza was standing at the school door. He opened it for Jamie with a smile.

"How are you?" he asked.

"OK," said Jamie.

"Good," said Mr. Karenza. "Look, come back in to my office for a minute, will you? I think you and I need to have a chat."

As they walked to the office, Mr. Karenza put his hand on Jamie's shoulder and said: "Your grandfather explained a little more about what's been happening in your life and I hope you know that everyone at this school is right behind you. But, that's not actually what I need to talk to you about..."

They sat down in the same chairs that they had occupied earlier that morning but now Mr. Karenza's face seemed different. He looked kinder.

"It seems I rather jumped the gun this morning," he said. "I didn't listen to your explanation. I owe you an apology for that."

Jamie nodded. He had no idea where all of this was coming from.

"Since you've been gone we've had a few conversations and made a couple of decisions. Tyler Forbes would like to step down from his starting spot in the team so that you take your place back. Drake Staunton has suggested that for this game, you be our captain. I would tend to agree with them. What do you say?"

Jamie stared at Mr. Karenza. Then he actually pinched himself to check that this was the real world. The same man who had banned him from playing for the school now wanted him back. As captain!

"So I'm back on the team?" Jamie asked. He needed to confirm this was actually happening.

"Yes," said Mr. Karenza. "And I know that you won't let me down. Now go and get your stuff—we don't want to be late!"

Jamie and Mr. Karenza shook hands and Jamie walked out of the office feeling half shell-shocked and half ecstatic. He was back in the game, ready to play the biggest match of his life, but his mind was teeming with all sorts of questions. How had all of this happened? It was fantastic news, but it made no sense whatsoever.

"Mr. Karenza?" said Jamie as he opened the door to leave the principal's office. He had to ask the question. He did not need charity from anyone. "What exactly did my grandpa say to you on the phone to make you put me back on the team?"

"No," said Mr. Karenza. "This has nothing to do with my conversation with your grandpa. It was the boys— Drake and Tyler—they came and told me what really happened on Friday. They said I couldn't punish you for something that was their fault."

"Really?" said Jamie. "OK..."

He shook his head and walked outside.

Could this day get any stranger?

13

Agent Johnson

"Enjoy the game," Hugo Bogson said as Jamie waited to get on the bus. "Do us proud."

"Sure will," smiled Jamie.

He assumed that would be the end of the conversation but Hugo was still standing there, shifting anxiously from side to side. He clearly had something further he wanted to say to Jamie.

"I had to tell them who you were, Jamie," he said. "It was the only way. But don't worry. They won't blow your cover."

"What?" said Jamie, "What are you talking about?"

"It was the only way to get you back on the team."

"Hugo, please tell me what you are talking about right now!" Jamie demanded. He was getting frustrated and the bus was just about to leave for Stonecroft.

"Shhh!" said Hugo. "You'll draw attention to us…"

He pulled Jamie to one side and began whispering.

"When Mr. Karenza told everyone that you'd been taken off the team because you'd thrown the egg, I went up to Drake and Tyler and I told them straight. I told them that they were messing with the wrong guy. I told them that you were with the CIA.

"At first they actually doubted me. But I told them to think about it—to put the clues together. An American kid turns up in England. Out of nowhere. No explanation. He doesn't talk about his life. Doesn't mention his family. No one's ever been to his house. He's obviously had martial arts training… How else do you explain it? He's clearly here on a CIA mission. Now is that really the kind of kid that you want make an enemy of?

"They went white as ghosts. You should have seen them. They ran straight into the principal's office, confessed to him exactly what happened on Friday. They even admitted that they had stolen the syrup and eggs. They seriously begged him to put you back on the team and to make you captain!"

"That's crazy!" said Jamie. "Well, um… I guess thanks anyway, Hugo."

This kid was something else. Did he actually believe this CIA fantasy?

"No," said Hugo, tapping his nose and smiling. "Thank *you*. And, like I said, Drake and Tyler won't tell anyone. They know what will happen if they do. Your secret is safe, Agent Johnson. The mission is still live."

Jamie shook his head. It was all too much.

"Oh!" said Hugo as Jamie boarded the team bus. "Would you please do one thing for me?"

"Sure," said Jamie. No matter which way he looked at it, he did owe Hugo one.

"The next time you see the President... will you just tell him Hugo Bogson says hi?"

14

Blood and Sweat

"Nearly there," said Mr. Karenza, as the battered old Wheatlands school bus chugged up a long, private road. On either side of the road, rows of tall, graceful trees led the way towards a huge mansion looming in the distance.

It had only taken the boys and girls of Wheatlands Primary School about ten minutes to get across town, but in that time, Jamie had seen a different way of life emerge in front of him.

The streets where he lived and went to school were small and cramped. The dark, old houses had all been built so close together that they looked to Jamie like they were leaning on each other, sheltering themselves from the cold.

Looking out the window, Jamie noticed how the homes started to grow in size, the streets became wider, and the grass grew greener.

Now, as the gravel crunched underneath the tires of the bus, Jamie stared up at the building ahead. He knew it must be Stonecroft School.

He took in every detail: the huge white pillars that seemed to hold up the massive mansion, the gigantic arched windows that offered a tantalising glimpse inside. Every element of the building—including the Latin words that had been carved by hand into the stone—seemed to be immaculate. Fit for a king.

Jamie's mouth hung open. This wasn't a school. It wasn't even a mansion. It was a palace.

Mr. Karenza stopped the bus and got out. Nearby, a gardener was planting a bunch of astonishingly beautiful plants into what looked like prize-winning flower beds.

Mr. Karenza shook the gardener's hand as though they were old friends while the boys and girls of Wheatlands stepped down off the bus and into a different world. Jamie honestly expected a member of the British royal family to appear at any moment.

Even the parking lot was something to behold. It was brimming with a collection of the snazziest, most expensive cars that Jamie had ever seen! A brand new Rolls Royce caught his eye in particular, complete with a chauffeur sitting in the front. Jamie figured these cars must belong to the rich parents who had no doubt come today to watch their kids play today.

For a second, Jamie thought of his own mom and her beat up old car which was parked, immobile, in front of their house. It hadn't worked for weeks but they didn't have the money to fix it. Did that make him any less of a person compared to these Stonecroft kids, with their Rolls Royces and their chauffeurs?

"OK, we've got to go now," said Alex Crawford, nudging Jamie as she got off the bus, a look of excited determination on her face.

"I'll see you after the game," she smiled. "And you better keep to your half of the deal!"

"You bet," said Jamie.

As captains, they had made a deal that they would do absolutely everything in their power as human beings to make sure that they *both* got back on that bus as winners.

"Blood and sweat," Alex had said. "Whatever it takes."

"Whatever it takes," Jamie repeated. He liked this girl's style.

The one thing that Jamie didn't tell Alex—he wanted it to be a surprise—was that today he was hoping to do something very special, something that no ten-year-old kid could be expected to do on a soccer field.

Today, Jamie was hoping to score the winning goal with a bicycle kick. Ever since he saw those videos last night, he hadn't stopped visualizing himself scoring an unbelievable goal. He knew he could do it. He knew it would make people sit up and take notice.

Hugo Bogson's CIA delusions earlier were obviously far-fetched, but he had been absolutely right about one thing. Jamie Johnson *was* on a mission. But it had nothing to do with the CIA. It was far more important than that. He was on a mission to start his soccer career.

15

Controlling the Beast

"Hello, welcome to Stonecroft," said a player from the opposition, as Jamie jogged out on to the field.

He was pretty much the biggest boy Jamie had ever seen. He looked more like he should be playing rugby—a kind of old–fashioned, English version of football—than soccer.

"My name's Sebastian Forde," the giant said politely, shaking Jamie's hand. "Listen, I've just lost one of my contact lenses. I was wondering if you could maybe help me find it?"

"Sure," said Jamie, surprised at how nice this Sebastian boy seemed. On the way to the game, Alex had warned Jamie that some of the Stonecroft kids were sly but this Sebastian seemed genuinely nice. Maybe these rich kids weren't so bad. Perhaps Jamie could even become friends with a couple of them... and go for a ride in their parents' Rolls Royces!

Jamie got down and started looking in the grass for the contact lens. He was really good at finding things, so he was sure he would be able to help Sebastian find his lens.

"Oh, my name's Jamie, by the way," he said, looking up at Sebastian, who, for some reason, wasn't looking for the contact lens himself. "If you're wondering about the accent, I'm from the State–"

Thump! Sebastian Forde kicked Jamie really hard in the back, sending him tumbling over on to the ground.

"What did you do that for?" Jamie yelled. His back really hurt. "I was just trying to—"

"I don't even wear contact lenses, you moron!" Sebastian howled with laughter. "And that's only the first time I'm gonna kick you today!"

"What's your problem?" said Jamie, getting up. He looked around for some backup, but everyone else was still in the locker room getting ready.

"You're my problem!" shouted Sebastian, leering over him. "Oh, are you standing up now? I couldn't even tell! Why are you so small then? Is your dad tiny too?!"

"Don't talk about my dad!" Jamie snarled. "You don't know anything about my dad!"

Jamie was so angry. The beast of his rage was demanding to be let out of its cage. But he managed to control himself. He was captain today. People were counting on him and he couldn't let them down.

"Ha! Ha! Must have hit a nerve!!" laughed Sebastian, walking back to the locker rooms. "Say hi to your tiny dad for me! See you out on the field!"

Jamie watched him go.

*You **will** see me out on the field*, he said to himself. *And you'll pay.*

16

Kick-off

Jamie stood in the middle of the perfect Stonecroft soccer field and watched the referee bring the whistle to his mouth.

This field, this setting, was perfect. It was fit to host a World Cup Final, let alone a school match between 22 ten-year-olds.

Jamie took a deep breath and held it in his chest. As he looked Sebastian Forde dead in the eye, he felt his pulse quicken and a sudden shot of adrenaline fire into his veins.

For a second, Jamie felt Mike's presence. He imagined what Mike would be saying to him now if he were here: "Trust your instincts. Trust your skill. Show them who you are."

Jamie nodded and jumped into the air.

Then the referee blew the whistle.

The match had kicked off.

* * * *

STONECROFT 1 : 1 WHEATLANDS
A. SHAH, 7   K. TALBOT, 16
30 MINS PLAYED

The game was only thirty minutes old but Jamie had to admit it. This was already the toughest match he had ever played.

Since he had come to England and joined the Wheatlands team, they had won every single game they had played. Normally Jamie just had to switch on his soccer computer and, within ten minutes, he'd scored four goals and pretty much won his team the game. With him on the wing and the school's speedy striker, Kane Talbot, in attack, they blew most teams away.

But today was different. Today, Wheatlands had come up against a team that were just as good as they were, if not better. Stonecroft was big, strong and well organized. They had one or two players who could kick the ball huge distances and three or four more who were capable of playing quick, slick passing soccer. It was going to be a seriously close game and everyone knew it.

Stonecroft took an early lead when their striker outpaced the entire Wheatlands back line before sending a clever chip over the goalkeeper and into the net.

All the assembled Stonecroft supporters—teachers, parents, brothers and sisters—celebrated the goal in crazy English style.

"What a stonking good finish!" they cried, waving their scarves above their heads.

"What an absolute belter!" they cheered in their posh accents.

Jamie had never even heard some of these words before.

But then, like any good team, Wheatlands hit back quickly. Jamie dribbled past four players and set up Kane Talbot, who equalized with a curling, trademark shot into the top corner.

Mr. Karenza leapt into the air to celebrate.

"You beauty!" he shouted, pumping his fist. "Great strike, Kane! Awesome dribble, Jamie! Come on, let's get another one!"

Winning this game seemed to mean as much to him as it did to his players.

But, since then, the game had been really tight.

Even Jamie was finding it hard to make an impression. Sebastian Forde was getting in his way.

He was tracking Jamie wherever he went, and if he wasn't putting in dangerous, crunching tackles, he was taunting and teasing Jamie with his trash talk. It was as if he really hated Jamie, even though this was the first time they had ever met each other.

"Hey, Yank, where did ya get those cleats? The thrift shop? Can't you afford a real pair?" Forde smirked as he made a run past Jamie towards Wheatlands' goal. Didn't he know that defenders were supposed to stay at the back?

Jamie hadn't reacted to any of Sebastian's jibes yet. He just had to be patient. He knew his time would come. Then he would show Sebastian what true talent was. Show him that skill was way more powerful than brute forc—

Suddenly the ball rebounded to Sebastian, who was standing 35 yards from Wheatlands' goal. Sebastian powered forward, controlling the ball firmly on his chest. It bounced up above his head and then, as it dropped, out of nowhere Sebastian pelted a ferocious left-foot volley at the goal. It was an awesome strike... and it was on target!

Jamie couldn't bear to watch. As soon as the ball was struck, his soccer computer told him this was a goal.

It shot like a rocket straight into the top corner.

Sebastian Forde, the big, stupid, thuggish defender, had just scored an unbelievable solo goal. And didn't he know it...

STONECROFT 2 : 1 WHEATLANDS

A. SHAH, 7   K. TALBOT, 16
S. FORDE, 31

"Come on!!" Sebastian shouted, his cheeks burning red with glory. He'd raced over to the corner flag and kicked it out of the ground.

"What do you think about that?!" he roared at the Wheatlands players. "You're on our turf now! Time to show some respect!"

17

Programmed to Play

STONECROFT 2 : 1 WHEATLANDS

A. SHAH, 7   K. TALBOT, 16
S. FORDE, 31

34 MINS PLAYED

Wheatlands was losing.

Jamie hated losing at anything. It didn't matter what it was: a game of cards, chutes and ladders, a computer game. When people told him it was how he played the game that mattered, not winning or losing, Jamie looked at them like they were nuts.

Whatever Jamie did, he had to win at everything. Losing just started a rage within him. A rage which could only be calmed with a win. Proof that he was the best.

Now, as the ball bounced towards him, Jamie knew what he had to prove. He knew it was time for him to make his move.

He gathered the ball and went on a run.

With the ball at his feet, Jamie's mind instantly rid itself of all the clutter that normally littered it. Thoughts of home, of his mom, of his dad, all dissolved. Now, as he ran down the wing, Jamie's brain was clear and free. Free for soccer. Programmed to play. Set to score.

Jamie turned on his turbo sprint and raced forward with the speed of a panther.

He sped past three players and was heading right for the heart of the Stonecroft defense when Sebastian Forde slashed him down with a violent foul.

Jamie was down. But not for long.

Because now he had exactly what he wanted.

A free kick.

* * * *

Jamie stood and faced the ball straight on. Then he took three steps back, stood up to his full height and puffed out his chest. He took a few deep breaths as he decided exactly what he wanted to do with this free kick.

It was a decent way out—22 yards from goal—so Jamie

knew he had to go for swerve and power rather than curl and accuracy.

He stared hard at the ball. He was thinking about Luiz Rodriguez. Rodriguez was a Portuguese winger and the best free kick taker in the world.

When he had watched Rodriguez's free kicks on YouTube, Jamie noticed that he never used a full follow-through. Rodriguez punched his cleat ferociously through the ball but then, as soon as possible after he had made contact, he brought his foot back down to the ground. The way Rodriguez struck the ball forced it to move in a way that no other technique could replicate.

Now it was Jamie's turn to give it a try.

Jamie took a final deep, determined breath, followed by three powerful strides towards the ball. Then he hit it with the maximum force his body possessed.

All the players on the field—and even the referee—were hypnotized by the movement of the ball in the air. They watched it arc towards its target.

Thwack! The ball hit the goalkeeper's right-hand post, halfway up! Now it was spinning furiously across the goal-line. Was it going to go in? Or was it—thud!

It hit the other post, and bounced out.

Initially, the players didn't react. They were so confused by the ball hitting both posts but still not going in that they didn't move. Every player, that is, apart from Kane Talbot.

Like any top striker, Kane Talbot was a natural born predator. His attacking instincts set in as soon as the ball hit the first post, hoping to hungrily snap up any rebound. He pursued the ball smoothly and swiftly, catching up with it in an instant before gobbling up the chance with a quick, powerful close-range strike.

STONECROFT 2 : 2 WHEATLANDS

A. SHAH, 7 **K. TALBOT, 16, 39**
S. FORDE, 31

Even though it was Talbot's name on the score sheet, Jamie still raised his arms proudly above his head in triumph. He knew how important his free kick had been to the goal. And he was not the only one.

Suddenly Jamie felt his whole body being hoisted into the air.

"What a free kick!" Drake Staunton was shouting. He and Jamie started screaming in disbelief and Drake lifted Jamie four feet off the ground.

Then, as they recovered their senses, the two boys looked at each other for a second, clearly embarrassed to have found themselves hugging when they had spent the last three months being archenemies.

Still, this was a crucial battle, and today, they were both members of the same tribe.

18

Moment of Truth

STONECROFT 2 : 2 WHEATLANDS

A. SHAH, 7   K. TALBOT, 16, 39
S. FORDE, 31

40 MINS PLAYED

There were now just ten minutes left in the match and both teams were piling forward in search of the winner. Glory was there for the taking, for whomever could find the final goal.

Jamie was desperate to get on the scoresheet himself and win the game for Wheatlands. He felt he still had a big role to play in this match.

But as time ticked on, it was Stonecroft who looked

more and more likely to score a goal.

They had a corner kick.

"You all go up," Sebastian Forde ordered his Stone-croft teammates. "Don't worry about the ugly little American; I'll handle him!"

Ugly?! Jamie truly hated this boy. If he could just get on to the ball, he knew he could tear Sebastian Forde to shreds. But, right now, the action was all happening at the other end of the field.

As the corner kick whipped into the center of the area, Drake Staunton and one of the Stonecroft players rose to contest it in the air. It was a 50-50 tussle, and although the Stonecroft player made the first connection with the ball, they clashed heads badly. It sounded like two coconuts being crashed together.

Jamie saw the Stonecroft player slump to the ground. He looked like he was in really bad shape—he hadn't even put his hands out to cushion his fall—but the ball had been cleared straight to Jamie...

With everyone committed to the corner, suddenly Wheatlands had a two-on-one breakaway. Jamie Johnson and Kane Talbot were tearing upfield together, with only Sebastian Forde in their way.

Jamie knew that now was the time. Time to let his talent come tumbling out.

With the ball at his feet, Jamie was ready to take Sebastian Forde head on.

He burst forward, travelling at his very top speed, juking left and right, always keeping the ball tight to him.

Now the tables had turned. Now Jamie was the one who was teasing Sebastian. His pace and control were mesmerizing the big defender.

Jamie turned this way and that way, each time slipping away from Sebastian's lunges. Jamie was like a wet bar of soap that Sebastian could never quite catch.

Then, having gained a crucial yard of space, Jamie looked up and stabbed a quick pass out to Kane Talbot on the right wing before racing into the penalty area himself. Now Sebastian was both outnumbered and surrounded. He didn't know which way to go.

"Play me back in, Kane!" Jamie demanded from his position at the far post. "I'm free!"

Kane Talbot swiftly slipped his foot under the ball and drifted a delicious cross into the air, destined to drop perfectly for Jamie.

Jamie watched as the ball floated towards him through the air.

His soccer computer switched on. His feet tingled with power and anticipation. This was his moment. The moment he had been imagining and preparing for. The moment to reveal his talent.

"He's going for the bicycle kick!" Jamie's teammates were shouting. They recognized the way he was setting himself up to take on the most spectacular skill in soccer.

But while his teammates were yelling at the top of their voices, Jamie's soccer senses had detected that something on the field was not quite right. The Stonecroft crowd on the sidelines had suddenly gone quiet.

In fact, they weren't even watching the game. They were pointing back towards the Wheatlands penalty area. There was worry on their faces. The Stonecroft player who had gone up for the header from the corner was still lying on the ground. He was unconscious.

The ball was still in the air. Jamie was focused and certain. He knew what he had to do. He jumped high into the air and, instead of attempting the bicycle kick, he actually caught the ball with both his hands.

Jamie remembered something important from when he used to play for his soccer team in Maine; they learned a lot about the dangers of concussions and the really bad injuries that can occur if they're not immediately treated.

He recognized that his opponent was in serious trouble because of the painful way he and Drake had clashed heads, and no matter what was at stake, this kid needed medical attention—even if that meant Jamie giving up the chance to score the game-winning goal.

"We have to stop the game," he shouted at the top of his voice. "That boy needs help!"

19

Touch of Class

STONECROFT 2 : 2 WHEATLANDS

A. SHAH, 7   **K. TALBOT, 16, 39**
S. FORDE, 31

FULL TIME

The game finished in a draw. Jamie had given up the chance to score the winning goal. The glory had been there in his grasp. One kick—one spectacular bicycle kick—and he could have won the game. He might even have got his name in the paper. He might even have been spotted by a Premier League club.

But he just couldn't do it. Not with that boy in so much trouble. As soon as he had stopped the game,

Stonecroft's trainer ran straight on the field, followed by a worried-looking man in a suit. They sprinted straight towards the stricken boy, instantly laying him on his side to get him breathing again.

Now, as he showered, got dressed and headed back out towards the Wheatlands bus for the journey home, Jamie wondered what Alex would make of it all when he told her. After all, he would not be getting back on that bus as a winner. While he was walking back to the bus, Jamie sensed a large presence looming over him.. He tensed his stomach muscles and prepared himself for conflict. If this was Sebastian Forde...

"My son and I owe you a huge debt of gratitude... Jamie, is it?"

Jamie looked up. It was the man in the suit who had run on to the field with the Stonecroft trainer to help the injured boy.

"No problem," said Jamie. "Is he OK? Looked like a bad one."

"Ollie's fine." The man smiled. He was wearing the nicest coat Jamie had ever seen. "Thanks to you. He'd been knocked clean out and his tongue was blocking his airway. If you hadn't done what you did, if we hadn't got to him so quickly—well, it doesn't bear thinking about. Look, how can I thank you?"

"It's fine," said Jamie. "Some things are more important than soccer. I'm just glad he's OK."

"No, really. I mean it—it was a real touch of class,

what you did," said the man, getting into his car. It was the Rolls Royce that Jamie had spotted earlier. "Trust me, I'll think of something."

Jamie stared at the car in awe.

"Hang on a minute," said the man, getting back out of his car. "I couldn't help but notice your accent. Are you American?"

"Sure am," smiled Jamie proudly.

"Great. And who's your favorite soccer team over here then, Jamie?"

"Hawkstone United," said Jamie. "All the way."

"I was hoping you might say that," nodded the man. "So where are you planning to watch the FA Cup game tomorrow?"

"I'm going to go to my grandpa's to watch it on TV. He's a huge Hawkstone fan too."

"Yup, you could do that," said the man. "Or you and your friends and family could come to the game as my guests. How would you like to be Hawkstone's junior captain for the match, Jamie?"

Jamie did a double take. He knew the junior captain got to meet the team, go into their locker room, maybe get a few autographs and even kick a ball around with some of the players. But this was all happening so fast.

"Oh," smiled the man. "Please excuse my rudeness. I should have introduced myself. My name's Tony. Tony Walsh. I'm the owner of Hawkstone United."

TUESDAY

A Proud Man

Jamie examined himself closely in the mirror. This was the face that 40,000 people would see on the field tonight.

Was he really ugly, like that boy Sebastian had said?

His mom had always said that he was handsome and that he would only get better looking the older he got. But then again, she was his mom. She would say that.

Back in the States, people said he looked like his dad and, when he'd been younger, that had made him proud. But now it just made him embarrassed. Now he wished he didn't have a dad. And, yet, at the same time, there wasn't a day that went by when Jamie didn't think about him, when he didn't wonder how his dad was coping in prison.

Jamie still could not understand what had driven his

dad to do it. They didn't need more money. They were just fine as they were. So why did he have to risk it and destroy their family, just for the sake of a few more lousy dollars?

Jamie could feel his chest start to tighten as his anger rose up within him. But no. He wasn't going to allow the problems of the past to ruin the present. This was now, not then. This was today. A special day.

The last 24 hours had been incredible. As soon as Jamie had got back on the Wheatlands bus, Mr. Karenza had stood up and made a little speech.

"What none of you are probably aware of is the fact that Stonecroft was actually the school that I went to," he revealed. "The whole reason I took this job, the whole reason that I work at Wheatlands is because I want to prove that money is not the only thing that matters. We can still produce great people from our school without the same kind of riches that they have. And, what Jamie Johnson did today—the level of intelligence and sportsmanship that he showed—well, you made me a proud man today, Jamie. Thank you."

Then, when Mr. Karenza explained that as a thank you to Jamie, Tony Walsh had invited his entire grade to come and watch the Hawkstone game the next night, the whole bus went wild.

Alex Crawford—who herself led the girls team to a brilliant two-nil victory—had even given Jamie a kiss on the cheek. The only problem was that everyone started teasing Jamie about it and his face had turned bright red with embarrassment!

It had been a wonderful 24 hours and now, as Jamie looked again at his face in the mirror, he saw his own reflection smiling back. It had been a rough few weeks, a rough few months. He'd almost forgotten what his own smile looked like.

"Do we have a Hawkstone junior captain in the house?!" someone suddenly shouted from downstairs.

Jamie smiled as he registered Mike's voice booming around the house.

"Come on, JJ, let's get this show on the road!"

JJ... Jamie repeated the nickname to himself. No one had ever called him that before. JJ for Jamie Johnson. *Yes*, he nodded. He kind of liked the ring of that.

Mike beamed with pride as Jamie appeared at the top of the stairs, already wearing his full Hawkstone uniform.

"Wow," said Mike. "Don't you look the part? I think it's time we got you to the stadium!"

21

Go for Your Dreams

Tony Walsh sent a special car that arrived right on time to take Jamie, his mom and Mike to the stadium. Meanwhile, Mr. Karenza was bringing the rest of Jamie's grade in the old school bus.

The car had brought Jamie's family right up to the front gates of the stadium. A nice lady was waiting to take Jamie down to the tunnel next to the field where he would walk out with the players and be introduced to the whole crowd by the stadium announcer. As he said goodbye to his mom and Mike, Jamie gave each of them a hug and promised to wave to them when he was out there.

Now, while he waited in the tunnel for the Hawkstone players to come out of their locker room, a feeling of disbelief fluttered through Jamie. Was he really here? In this stadium? At a Premier League soccer club?

"Hey, buddy," said Hawkstone captain Diego Medina, who was the first player out of the locker room. He shook Jamie's hand and said, "What's your name? I'm Diego."

Jamie almost laughed. He knew who Diego Medina was. Watching Diego play three days before had ignited Jamie's dream to be a soccer star. And now, here he was actually talking to Diego Medina, in real life!

"I'm Jamie," he said shyly. "Jamie Johnson."

"Nice to meet you, Jamie. Hey, that accent sounds familiar!"

"Yeah, I'm American too," smiled Jamie, trying to keep it as cool as he possibly could, given the circumstances. "And I want to be a soccer player when I'm older—just like you."

Diego Medina laughed and ruffled Jamie's hair. "Good for you, kid," he smiled. "Go for your dreams!"

Then the referee—who had a very bald head and very hairy legs—walked to the front of the line and shook hands with both captains. The smiles disappeared and serious expressions emerged. These were tough men. They were the leaders of their tribes.

"Ready, guys, here we go!" bellowed Diego Medina, banging the wall.

Then Diego Medina grabbed Jamie's hand and began the walk out of the tunnel towards the battlefield.

With every stride, the roar of the crowd got nearer and louder.

Now, as they walked out on to the field, the tidal wave of noise filled Jamie's ears.

At that moment, he couldn't imagine that anything else was happening in the world. It seemed that everyone on earth was here, shouting their heads off, waiting for the battle to commence!

There were cameras, commentators and 40,000 people all focusing their attention in Jamie's direction. And yet, as Jamie picked up a ball along the way, he felt no nerves whatsoever. Math tests made him nervous, not soccer.

As he took his first steps on the Hawkstone field, a set of words kept repeating themselves in Jamie's mind.

This thought seemed to be coming from every cell in his body: *"This is where I belong... This is where I'm meant to be."*

Right up until the last few days, Jamie would have done anything to get back to his old life in America but, now, here he was, in England, feeling like a soccer star.

There was nowhere else in the entire solar system he would rather be.

22

Caught Up in the Moment

"Jamie! Coin toss!" shouted Diego Medina.

He remembered Jamie's name! Diego Medina actually remembered Jamie's name!

As they walked to the center circle to toss the coin with the opposition, Jamie saw the look of steel in Diego's eyes, which said that he would stop at nothing to achieve victory. He thought of all the challenges this man must have overcome; he arrived in England as an unknown American, yet here he was, succeeding on one of soccer's grandest stages, the Premier League.

Determination, hard work, sacrifice. They were just words, just concepts. But Jamie would have to live by them every day if he was serious about wanting to emulate Diego's achievements.

"OK," said the stadium announcer, coming between

Jamie and Diego. "Do you want to come and have your shot at goal now, little man?"

"You bet!" said Jamie, following behind as the announcer half walked, half jogged towards the penalty area.

"OK," said the announcer picking up his microphone and checking his watch. "Just one quick shot, then we'll have to get you off the field and leave it to the professionals!"

The announcer cleared his voice, checked his hair and then spoke to the crowd.

"Good afternoon everybody!" he said, putting on his best *entertainer* voice, as his words boomed around the stadium.

"Hawkstone's junior captain this afternoon is a little lad called Jonny Johnson and he's come all the way from America! Let's give Jonny our support as he takes his shot on goal!"

The announcer stepped slightly to the side, leaving just enough room for Jamie to line up his shot.

Jamie wanted to correct the announcer, to tell him it was Jamie not Jonny! But he sensed that the man probably did not really care too much anyway. Who was Jamie to him? Just this week's junior captain.

Jamie took in a deep, long breath. He looked at the ball. Then he looked at the goalkeeper who was smiling at him, clapping his hands together. Normally, when the junior captains had a shot at goal, it was a measly, weak effort, barely strong enough to reach the goal line. The goalkeeper would often just let the ball go in to give the kid their special moment of pleasure; to allow them to say that they scored a goal in front of all those fans.

That wasn't what Jamie wanted. He wanted to score a goal in his own right. He wanted to get it into the net because it genuinely beat the keeper, not because the keeper let it in.

Jamie stared at the ball. It was resting just on the edge of the area. It was sitting there, begging to be hit.

His eyes went from the ball to the top corner of the net and back again. He ignored the fact that the announcer was practically standing in his way. He blocked out the sights and the sounds of everyone in the ground. He wasn't thinking about his family and his schoolmates being there, watching his every move.

This was just him and the ball.

Jamie took three, big, deliberate, steps backwards, loosened his neck by twisting it from side to side and rolled his shoulders back to relax his upper body.

He stood up, as tall as he possibly could and puffed out his chest. The preparation of his free kick routine was complete. Now it was time for the final, crucial, masterful element: the strike.

He took three swift strides towards the ball. He pulled his leg back with controlled, powerful aggression. He swung it forward at maximum speed and...kicked his own leg, painfully hard, tripping himself up and landing in a crumpled heap on the ground.

The ball hadn't even moved.

Jamie's heart ached with shame and he pounded the ground in frustration.

He could not even get up because his cleats were tangled in the wire of the announcer's microphone. His studs must have become caught up in the wire as he swept his cleat along the grass at the vital moment.

"Oh, what a shame!" said the announcer hurriedly untangling the wire and pulling Jamie to his feet as he spoke to the crowd.

"Oh well, there we go. Never mind!" he continued. "I guess we have to remember that soccer is still a relatively new sport over in America. Little Jonny did the best he could. Let's give him a big round of applause anyway!"

There were a couple of sympathetic claps and there were also some chuckles of laughter, as the fans shook their heads. Most of them were just glad it had not been them that had tripped over in front of 40,000 people.

The truth was, all of these people probably thought that *little Jonny Johnson* had never kicked a ball before in his life.

23

Forget You

"Hey! That wasn't fair!" Jamie appealed, tugging at the announcer's arm. "I only tripped because your wire was too close to the ball! Let me have another try!"

"No time, little man," said the announcer checking his watch again. "The match is about to kick off."

"Please!" begged Jamie. "It'll only take a second. I'll score this time—you just watch!"

"Do you understand English?!" snapped the announcer. "I said **NO**!"

Jamie took a step back. He shook his head.

That same ball was still there on the edge of the penalty area, still begging to be hit. But Jamie's time was up. He turned towards the tunnel, cursing his luck. He could not even bear to wave to his family and the kids from his school. They had all been there to watch this disaster.

He would never live it down.

"Typical spoiled American kid," the announcer muttered under his breath.

Suddenly Jamie stopped walking. Now, why did the announcer have to go and say a thing like that? Now he'd made Jamie angry. Very angry.

Forget you, Jamie thought to himself as he slowly turned around. *This is **my** time.*

Jamie glared directly at the announcer and then he walked straight back up to the ball on the edge of the area and flicked it into the air.

"Hey!" shouted the announcer. "What are you doing? I told you to get off the field!"

Jamie ignored him. It was time to show this guy who Jamie Johnson was. It was time to turn on the soccer computer. He zoomed in on the falling ball, controlling it perfectly on his chest, before heading it back up into the air...

Using every ounce of concentration in his body, Jamie processed the height, power, angle, trajectory and speed required to send the ball flying back over his head, and shooting like a rocket towards the goal. Then, at precisely the correct millisecond, he launched his body up off the ground to meet the ball and execute the strike.

Lying completely flat in the air, Jamie propelled his foot back over his head with ferocious power.

The contact was sweet and powerful, hard and accurate. As Jamie dropped to the ground, he didn't even have to look around. The computer was already analyzing the direction and accuracy of the strike. It was 100%. The bicycle kick was fully loaded.

Jamie's shot fired like a cannonball through the Hawkstone sky. It whistled as it sped towards the target. The goalkeeper—a professional, top tier athlete—initially went to save the ball but quickly aborted.

The strike was too quick. Too powerful. Too good.

The keeper simply stood, hypnotized, as the ball flew straight into the top corner of the net. Then, just for a moment before gravity took hold, the ball hovered in the most prized section of the goal, almost as though it wanted everyone to see.

This was a moment of pure soccer genius.

And it had been achieved by an American kid called Jamie Johnson.

24

The First Glimpse

The ball dropped to the ground, bounced once and then settled in the back of the net.

For a moment, there seemed to be complete silence.

Then, the sound of one, lone person applauding emerged.

It was Diego Medina.

He clapped loudly and proudly. He was walking towards Jamie, shaking his head.

"Man," he said, giving Jamie a fist-bump of respect. "You got some skills, kid. Maybe I will see you out here in a few years. Go for those dreams, Jamie."

As he walked towards the center spot to take the kick off for Hawkstone's big match, Diego Medina was still clapping. Except now, he wasn't alone.

The applause in the crowd started slowly at first—from just one group of school kids and their immensely proud teacher—but it was now quickly spreading throughout the stadium like a hungry fire...

"OK... um, well, then..." the announcer said to the crowd. "Yes, I guess our junior captain does deserve a little round of applause!"

But the fans were way ahead of the announcer. By now, the entire stadium was clapping for Jamie as the big screen above the goal replayed his stunning bicycle kick from a series of different angles, each one more impressive than the last.

"His name is Jamie Johnson, by the way," said the announcer, finally getting it right. "Remember that name."

"*One Jamie Johnson!*" sang the Hawkstone fans, their chant reverberating throughout the stadium. "*There's only one Jamie Johhhnson!*"

Jamie's heart burned with pride. He loved the feeling of being cheered on by so many people. He hoped this would never stop. This was what he wanted for the rest of his life. He turned to wave to the crowd in every corner of the ground.

Up in the corner of the stand, he saw his whole grade, led by Alex and Hugo, all standing up, clapping for him and waving. Jamie smiled at them and waved back. He could see they were proud of him. He could tell they accepted him as one of them now. Mission accomplished, as Hugo Bogson might have said.

Then Jamie spotted his grandpa. He knew just how much it meant to Mike to see his grandson down there on the same Hawkstone field that he had once played on. Playing for the club that he still loved.

Jamie understood now where his soccer computer came from. It was a gift from his grandpa. Jamie saluted Mike, who clenched his fist and beamed a giant grin back. They weren't grandpa and grandson. They were buddies. And they were about to go on an epic soccer journey together.

Finally, Jamie saw his mom. She had been through a lot. He knew she still cried sometimes at night but now, as she waved to him, she seemed to be crying happy tears. Jamie smiled and waved back to her. He was beginning to realize that, if the two of them stuck together, they would be just fine in the end. As long as they had each other, it didn't matter where in the world they lived—it would always feel like home.

As the appreciation for him got louder and louder, with almost every fan now roaring his name, Jamie leapt high into the air, punching his fist skyward. He had been through a lot too, but right now, he was happy. He was free. He was where he belonged.

And, yet, the truth was, even though these soccer fans were already in awe of Jamie Johnson's ability, they hadn't seen anything yet.

This boy was born to play soccer and, soon enough, he would show the world what he could do.

Acknowledgements

Huge thanks to Tim Gentles and Kevin Clark for their unwavering support throughout. And to everyone who has helped along the way: Jason Cox, William Major Bolitho, Lola Cashman, Vicky Toubian, Caitlin Krieck, Jennifer Ferguson, Evonne DeNome, Samantha Selby-Smith, Jason Sisneros, Dave Baldwin, George Baldwin, Hayley Katz, Chris Gerstle, Alex Stone, Matt Moran, Arnaldo Hase, Pedro Badur, Paulo Sivieri, Hazel Ruscoe, Andy Downer, Adina Popa, Loudoun County Public Schools, Brad Friedel, Gary Blumberg, Ben Levey, Cliff McCrath, Anson Dorrance, Erin Layne, Sari Rose, John O'Sullivan, Jeanie Foreman, Brett Rhodes, Adam Barnard, The British International School of New York, Toby Moynihan, Scott Debson, Remy Cherin, Corey Sinser, United Soccer Coaches, Gasch Printing, Phil Abbott, Jennon Bell Hoffman, Cecelia Powell, Bob Kawabe, Sasha Wilson, Elliott Moore, Phillip Glyn and Kristin Thrower.

Your inspiration and support has been invaluable.

TOP FIVE QUESTIONS
with Dan Freedman

1. What is it like writing about a kid who wants to be a soccer star?

Great. At one stage, even the best soccer players in the world were all just soccer-mad schoolkids! So we can all empathize with Jamie's dream of making it to the top.

2. Do you get much fan mail from your readers?

Yes, what with my website, emails, letters and social media, there are lots of ways for Jamie Johnson fans to get in touch with me and I always make sure I respond. Being an author, you tend to spend a fair bit of time writing on your own, so hearing from people who have read the books is always a brilliant moment. It makes all the hard work worth it! I got one email from a teacher at a school in the Himalayas. It just shows the power that books and stories have.

3. What's the best goal you've ever seen?

It genuinely is Marco van Basten's bicycle kick for Ajax v Den Bosch in 1986. Check it out!

4. What the best game you've ever seen live?

I was lucky enough to watch the World Cup Quarter Final: Brazil v England in Japan in 2002 and then fly home on the plane to London with the England players afterwards.
I'll never forget it...

5. What's your favorite thing about writing about Jamie Johnson and who is he based on?

I get to sit and daydream about soccer! That's my job! I also find Jamie very intriguing as a character. I always say that, with Jamie, you're never quite sure what he's going to do. Is he going to turn around, produce a sensational bit of skill and fire one in from 35 yards? Or is he going to lose his temper, do something he regrets and get himself sent off? Characters like that keep you guessing, which is great for the readers and the author. Jamie is partly based on me (we have a fair bit in common) and partly based on the great players I have been lucky enough to meet. I have taken a little bit from each of these players, added them to my own personality and experiences ... and the result is Jamie Johnson. Ultimately, I guess he is just the kind of player I would love to watch play soccer.

Read the first chapters from

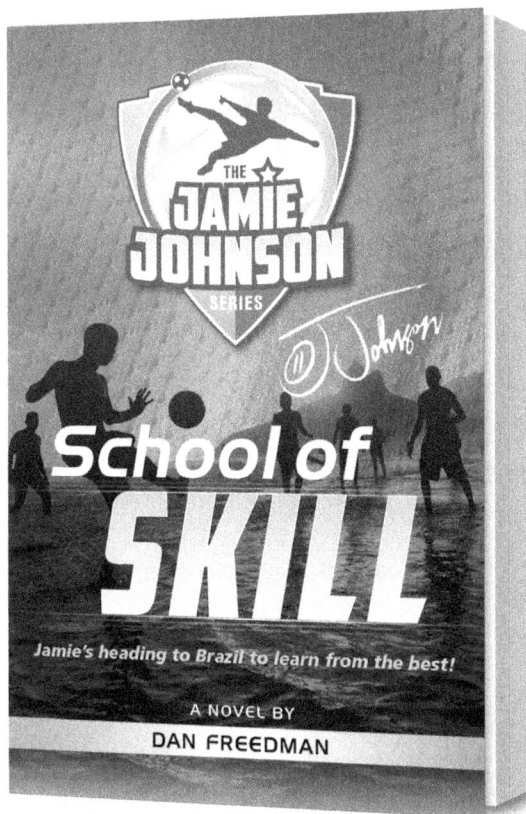

The Jamie Johnson Series
Available from www.jamiejohnson.soccer

A press conference is being held at Hawkstone United's stadium. A sharply dressed man walks through the door and into the room. It is full of photographers and journalists, all there to hear what he has to say.

The man sits down at the table and clears his throat. He knows what he is going to say. He spent last night preparing these words. He has been preparing for this moment his entire life. He pulls the microphone towards him and begins to speak.

"I want to say what an honor it is to be managing in the Premier League and, in particular, here at Hawkstone United," he explains.

His voice is cool, crisp, clear and confident.

"This is a dream come true for me."

What Makes You So Special?
Tuesday, April 29th

"Jamie Johnson!" Mr. Pratley shouted, his hot, smelly coffee breath roaring like a dirty hurricane into Jamie's face.

He grabbed Jamie's scribbled line-up of a Hawkstone United team with all his favorite players and, of course, J. Johnson as number 11, the left-winger.

This was far from the first time that Jamie had been caught playing fantasy soccer instead of listening. When it came to soccer, Jamie's brain was like a powerful computer, working out teams, angles, shots and passes…. But when it came to listening to Pratley, well, Jamie just seemed to turn off as soon as the man started talking. It drove Pratley wild with rage.

"Do you have any idea how many kids have been

through this school and claimed that they were going to be a professional soccer player when they grew up? Hundreds…thousands!"

Mr. Pratley was now tearing up Jamie's sheet into as many little pieces as possible. The more he ripped the page into smaller and smaller pieces, the redder his face became and the wider his eyes bulged.

Jamie did not respond. He couldn't. It was taking every ounce of his focus not to burst into laughter. All he could do was stare at the big green booger that was hovering, tantalizingly loose, from the end of Mr. Pratley's nostril. It was a beauty: wet and sticky, yet still hard enough to be absolutely ripe for the picking.

"And of those thousands of kids," Pratley continued, the redness now rising from his face into his big, shiny, balding head, "who ALL thought they were going to be professional soccer players, who ALL thought they were God's gift to the game—just like you, no doubt, do—have you any idea how many of them did it? How many of them became pro soccer players?"

Jamie shook his head. He noticed the more worked up Pratley got, and the louder he shouted, the more the booger began to wobble. It was as though it was dancing to the beat of Pratley's anger.

Pratley walked to the front of the classroom and chucked the remnants of Jamie's sheet into the trash. Then he turned and marched back towards Jamie.

The closer he got, the better the view Jamie had of

the booger. It was now doing something amazing. When Pratley breathed out, the booger poked further out of his nose, as if it were waving to the world. And when he breathed in, it returned slightly further back up his nostril. It appeared to be on some kind of invisible string.

"None!!" barked Pratley. "Not one of those kids became professional soccer players! So, I would like you to tell me why you think you are any different."

Jamie looked at his best friend, Alexandra—or, Alex, as everyone knew her—for help. She shook her head. *Don't talk back.* That's what she was signalling with her eyes. And she was right. This was a regular occurrence between Jamie and Mr. Pratley.

For some reason, Jamie had the ability to get under Pratley's skin more than any other kid in the whole school. Normally the kids found it hysterical, but right now, they had reached the danger zone; one more word from Jamie and Pratley just might explode.

Of course there were plenty of things Jamie could have said; lots of arguments he could have put forward to explain why he believed that, one day, he would become a professional soccer player....

He was by far the best player in the school, and he got all his talent from his grandfather, who, had it not been for the injury, would easily have been one of Hawkstone's greatest-ever players. Jamie trained and practiced every single day because he wanted to become not just a professional soccer player but one of the best players in the world....

But he didn't say anything. Alex was right. They both knew that whenever Jamie answered back, it only made Pratley even angrier. The best course of action Jamie could take now would be to say nothing. Nothing at all.

And so Jamie just shrugged his shoulders and stayed quiet.

"Answer me, Johnson!" yelled Pratley. "Or I'll keep you in here for the entire lunch period by yourself. What makes you think you're so special? What makes you think you've got something that all those other kids didn't?"

Pratley's face was now just an inch from Jamie's. The booger was smack bang in front of Jamie's eyes. It was moving in and out of the teacher's nose, perfectly in time with Pratley's pants of fury.

Out of the corner of his eye, Jamie saw Alex turn away. Her body was quivering. She had seen it too, and had started laughing without making any noise.

Jamie could feel it coming inside him too. It was rising up through his body like an unstoppable river from his lungs into his throat, and now it was at his mouth. The laughter could not be controlled for very much longer.

"For the very last time, Johnson! Why do you think you are better than any of them?"

"I don't know..." Jamie finally stuttered. The laughter was already leaking out. He knew he was going to get into trouble anyway, so he thought he might as well make it worth it.

"**Snot** really for me to say!"

2

The Day of Destiny

"We'll know tomorrow!" shouted Alex, grabbing Jamie by his shirt and dragging him out of lunch.

"Know what?" he asked, laughing as she dragged him along all the way to the auditorium.

"TOMORROW!" she repeated, pushing him face to face with the sheet of paper on the bulletin board that announced their day of destiny.

Teachers vs
6th Grade Students

SOCCER
MATCH

· · · · · · · · · · ·

The date for this game has been confirmed!

Details will be announced
at assembly tomorrow.

Jamie stared at the board.

The note was about the soccer game that he had being looking forward to all year, the match between the teachers of Wheatlands Primary School and the sixth grade students. When Jamie first moved to the UK a little over a year ago, he thought it was strange that the school was for first through sixth graders.

But now that he was a sixth grader, on top of the food chain at Wheatlands, Jamie knew this game was going to be huge. Maybe the biggest game of his life.

Jamie and Alex gazed at the Wheatlands Primary School Soccer Trophy. Gleaming like treasure, it stood, as always, in its special cabinet in the auditorium. It remained there for the whole year until, on the day of the game itself, the principal, Mr. Karenza, removed the prize from the cabinet and handed it to the winning captain to lift into the air.

Alex, who had been at Wheatlands since first grade, regaled Jamie with horror stories of the previous sixth graders' embarrassing losses at the hands of the teachers. Even though Alex was already the best goalkeeper in the school by fourth grade, she could only look on helpless from the sidelines as the teachers racked up win after win, year after year.

But this year Jamie and Alex were in sixth grade. Now it was their chance to play and put things right, to finally give the teachers a taste of their own medicine.

They had promised themselves that, in this game, things would be different, that this would be their year.

However, just one look at the wooden board—on which was engraved the results of all the previous matches—made clear how difficult the task was that lay ahead.

And it also named the teacher who would be standing in their way.

Teachers vs Sixth Grade Students
GAME RESULTS

Teachers 11–8 Students	Winning Captain: C Pratley
Teachers 6–4 Students	Winning Captain: C Pratley
Teachers 4–4 Students	Match abandoned
Teachers 8–1 Students	Winning Captain: C Pratley
Teachers 7–3 Students	Winning Captain: C Pratley
Teachers 5–2 Students	Winning Captain: C Pratley
Teachers 9–6 Students	Winning Captain: C Pratley
Teachers 5–3 Students	Winning Captain: C Pratley
Teachers 7–6 Students	Winning Captain: C Pratley
Teachers 6–4 Students	Winning Captain: C Pratley
Teachers Students	Winning Captain:

3

10,000 Hours

"Come on," said Alex. "Spit it out."

She and Jamie were walking home from school together, as they did every day, kicking an old soda can between them along the street.

Jamie shook his head and glanced at his pale legs moving next to Alex's light brown ones. He always wished that he could have skin like hers. His was white and pasty and never ever tanned. If he spent even a moment in the sun, he got red and burnt all over, whereas Alex's skin looked perfect all year round.

Jamie looked away as she tried to get him to open up, and shook his head again. Sometimes, he didn't like to talk. Even to Alex.

"Look," she said. "You always tell me eventually, so why don't we just skip past the silent bit and get to the talking part?"

Jamie stared at her. Alex constantly surprised and impressed him. It had been the same since the day he met her, she was one of the only kids in fifth grade that bothered to get to know Jamie when he joined Wheatlands after he moved from the United States.

They connected straight away, forging a strong partnership. Jamie felt out of place in a new school and a new country, and even though he looked like most of the other kids, he certainly didn't talk like them. Even some of the vocabulary was different. Right now, both he and Alex were wearing sneakers, but here in England they were called trainers.

From the start, Alex seemed to want to help Jamie settle in. She said her granddad had always told her that when he was a young man coming over to the UK from Antigua, it was the people that had been kind to him and shown him the ropes, that he had never forgotten.

"I'll show you around," Alex had said to Jamie on his first day in school, looking at him with uncanny brown-green eyes through her deep brown locks. Jamie had instantly known that this girl was special, and when he found out that she was also fanatical about soccer, well, it was game over. With Jamie being an attacker and Alex being a brilliant goalkeeper, they practiced their soccer together every day, challenging each other to reach the highest levels they could.

Not that Alex was just someone for Jamie to kick around with after school. She was his first true friend in the UK. Somehow, Alex made Jamie feel comfortable no matter what. Often Jamie felt that she knew him better than he knew himself.

"It's that stuff Pratley was saying today," Jamie began, "that I'm no different than all the other kids that wanted to be pro soccer players and didn't make it. I know I was laughing and stuff, but I can't get it out of my head."

"You're not still worried about Pratley, are you?" Alex said. "Just because he's a teacher doesn't mean he knows everything. My dad always says that the people that make the rules aren't any better than the rest of us."

"Yeah," said Jamie, "but what if Pratley's actually right? What if I am no better than the others?"

"OK. So what are you going to do about it?" she responded immediately.

"What?" said Jamie. He was shocked by her abruptness and missed his kick of the can.

"Well, you can either keep worrying about it, thinking you're no better than everyone else, or, if being a pro soccer player really is your dream, you can start making it happen, doing something to give yourself that extra edge."

Jamie smiled at her. Alex was the cleverest person he knew but he had no idea what she was talking about.

"How many hours did your grandpa Mike say you'd have to practice if you wanted to become a professional soccer player?" she asked.

"10,000," said Jamie. It was one of the many pieces of advice Mike had given Jamie about soccer over the last year. Mike said that the top players only looked so good because they had practiced so long and from a very young age.

10,000 hours seemed like a huge amount but, for Jamie, every second he spent playing soccer was pure joy.

"Cool," said Alex, flicking the can into the air. "So let's get to the park and get practicing!"

And with that she volleyed the can all the way over to the other side of the street, where it looped perfectly into a nearby dumpster.

Jamie breathed a little more easily. He still felt hurt and worried by Pratley's comments but, at the same time, having Alex's support always helped.

Jamie was an electrifyingly quick left-winger and Alex was a brave, athletic goalkeeper. Together they made a pretty good pair, which was lucky because they both knew that, if they were going to stand any chance of beating the teachers and claiming that gleaming trophy at the end of the year, they would need to be part of the best students' team in the history of Wheatlands Primary School.

Follow Jamie's journey to the top! Don't miss the next book in the series:

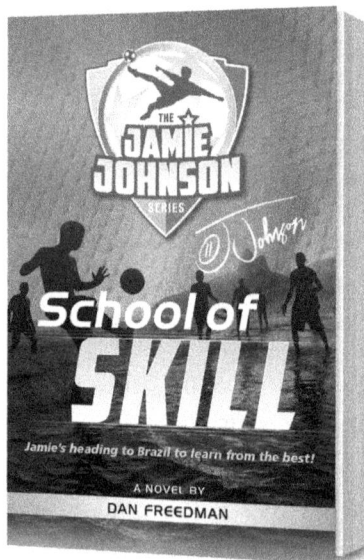

Visit **www.jamiejohnson.soccer** for the latest news on the next installment of The Jamie Johnson Series.